The
Blind Date
Survival Guide

A Practical and Funny (Well, Practically
Funny) Step-by-Step Guide to Meeting the
Person of your Dreams.

Jeff Nagel

Blockbuster Publications, Inc.
Greenvale, NY

Published by: Blockbuster Publications, Inc.
P.O. Box 415
Greenvale, NY 11548

Printed in the United States of America

10 9 8 7 6 5 4 3 2 1

This book can be ordered by mail direct from the publisher. Please use the enclosed order form at the back of this book or send $9.95 plus $2 postage and handling to Blockbuster Publications, Inc.

The Blind Date Survival Guide

12/12/05

Bill,

Always remember ...

life is too important to take

seriously !

Illustrations by Jessica Robison
Illustrations conceived by Jeff Nagel

To my parents

who met on a blind date

Acknowledgements

This book was made possible by the collective efforts of five people.

I thank David Penzell for advising me to write this book and helping me develop the first draft, Bob Finkle for talking me into going on my first blind date (I still haven't forgiven him), Josh Logan, my publisher, for all those long nights of editing, and my Mom for buying the first 200 copies.

And special thanks to William Kaufman, whose constant support and advice made this book a reality.

Dedication

This book is dedicated to the following people for being research subjects and supplying source material:

Beth Ann Wendy Rhonda Andrea Jackie Pam Barb Roberta Judy Rhonda Patty Amy Judy Caryl Erica Eileen Cheryl Rosy Cheryl Betsy Kim Carol Cindy Jody Audrey Robbin Claudia Pam Laurie Nancy Tammy Michelle Barbara Rhonda Leah Michelle Rona Janet Beth Carol Nancy Judy Helene Judy Nancy Marcy Cindy Rachel Diane Andrea Lauren Lisa Cindy Amy Elizabeth Linda Leslie Emily Judith Laura Sue Dena Robin Linda Kim Gail Judy Ellen Ruth Debbie Rachel Michelle Debbie Rachel Anne Jasmine Judy Donna Ellen Kristy Kim Sandy Debbie Lisa Lori Lisa Judy Amy Amy Debbie Dana Laurie Nancy Lynn Jayne Wendy Beth Laurie Janice Michelle Ellen Liz Andrea Denise Suzanne Janet Margie Lisa Lisa Nancy Michele Debbie Suzy Liz Leslie Lisa Lori Sue Robin Jill Risa Debbie Suzanne Liz Sandy Cheryl Faith Debbie Gail Kim Nancy Wendy Randy Judy Katie Diane Suzanne Julie Stacey Denise Ogie Jane Jayu Terry Karen Jenny Jane Nancy Fran Michele Margie Irene Gigi Alice Jan Shari Wendy Abby Karen Rhonda Linda Sue Nancy Shari Lauri

Contents

Preface

Do you need this book? Take a minute to answer these four simple questions and find out:

- Are you tired of laughing *at* your dates instead of with them?
- Do you still get nightmares thinking about the only blind date you ever had?
- Do you have friends that say,"I hope you don't mind, but I met a nice person on the bus today and I gave out your phone number?"
- Would you rather have a root canal than go on a blind date?

KEY: If you answered YES to any of the above questions, you need this book.

Introduction

From the day I broke up with my girlfriend I realized it wouldn't be easy meeting women again. (OK, so I broke up with her *after* she threw me out of the apartment and told me never to return. Do you want to nitpick or can I finish this story?) Anyway, having been out of circulation for a couple of years, I forgot all my old pick-up lines, which is just as well, since they didn't work then either.

So I figured that blind dating was my best bet, and I pursued it without the advice of friends or experts. I made numerous mistakes in the beginning, all in the name of research so other poor schnooks—both male and female—wouldn't have to. After the number of blind dates reached 137 I decided to write a book to pass along my experience (and that of 150 people I interviewed) to those of you who are either a novice at the blind dating game or would just like to improve your skills.

I organized this guide in a step-by-step format and indexed it in a small, pocket-sized edition so that you could bring it with you on a blind date and refer to the appropriate sections quickly, as the need arises. (OK, so you need a really big pocket).

For example, you just met your date, who has the vocabulary of a rock. You ascertain this when the date fails to respond to the usual trick question: "Hi! How are you?"

Obviously, you should change the plans of going to a restaurant for a quiet evening of enlightening conversation. So, you pretend to sneeze and, as you do, turn around and reach for your handkerchief in your back pocket. But, instead of withdrawing the hanky, you cleverly whip out your indexed copy of The Blind Date Survival Guide. Turning to the section on where and when to go on the date, you decide to go to a movie instead, where dates will not have to open their mouths except to shove popcorn in. Once again, this guide comes to the rescue.

This book is intended to prevent you from spending a long evening with someone whose goal in life is to be the head toll taker on the Golden Gate bridge or taking your life's savings and spending it on a dinner for two. In your parents' day you could take out a date for a 50¢ ice cream. Today, that same ice cream date in a city like New York or Los Angeles could cost you over $30 between tolls, gas, parking, and designer Gelato.

I wrote this book assuming the worst will happen (or has already happened) on your blind dates. If the date turns out to be the person of your dreams, throw out this book. You should be able to handle that solo. However, for the greater percentage of blind dates that turn out to be "an experience," it is useful to know in advance how to make them as painless as possible.

Finally, this book has another purpose. Once published, all the major talk show hosts will want me to appear on their shows. With all the publicity I'll get, maybe I can meet women without going on blind dates.

SECTION I:

What Is a Blind Date?

Chapter 1
The Blind Date Defined

"I don't care what the wizard said; I am <u>not</u> going out with your cousin!"

Definitions

Webster's Definition:

- *Blind Date* n: a date between persons of opposite sex not previously acquainted; also: either of the persons.

Alternative Definitions:

- Someone you would not go out with under normal circumstances.

- Someone who would not go out with you under normal circumstances.
- Someone who knows the theme song to *The Love Boat* by heart.

While Webster's definition appears quite clear-cut, there are circumstances where the definition gets a little hazy. For example, suppose you are at a party and meet someone for a moment. You didn't get a chance to talk to that person...you were casually introduced in passing.

Three months later a friend of yours wants to fix you up with that person you met briefly at the party, but you can't remember what the person looked like. Is this considered a blind date? Is this considered a second date? Do you even care?

History of the Blind Date

Most people believe that blind dating began in the early 1900's. Actually, blind dating has been documented back to the days of the cavemen.

In 300 B.C. Og had nothing better to do on a Saturday night than watch reruns of "The Love Dugout Canoe" and chase wild Brontasaurus. He was getting tired of the "single cave thing" when his best friend Ug gave him the name of his sister Grunt. Og threw her a message on a rock and they met for a Teradactil burger. That was the first known blind date.

In the middle ages different kingdoms were always fighting with each other to expand their territories. After years of bloodshed King Henry VII came up with the idea of "arranging a marriage" between his son

Henry VIII and a princess Ann from a warring kingdom. The king felt this marriage would create a bond between the two kingdoms and thus, end the war. The plan would have worked out great, except Henry VIII had his wife executed. As a matter of fact, all of his wives, whom he executed, were originally blind dates.

What Is a Blind Date?

Chapter 2
Your Dating IQ

*"I told you before I wouldn't go out with you even if you **were** the last man on earth."*

Read through the following situations and choose how you would react in each one.

1. You ask your waitress for her phone number and she tells you she has a boyfriend. You should...
   - ☐ a) ask how big he is.
   - ☐ b) challenge him to a duel.
   - ☐ c) ask for a different table.
   - ☐ d) ask her if she has any friends.

2. You are at a party and your best friend introduces you to her date to whom you are very attracted. You should...

□ a) steal your friend's date.

□ b) be honorable and respect your friendship.

□ c) ask her if you can take her date to your summer house for the weekend as "just friends."

3. You ask Susan out for a date three times and each time she tells you that she has to wash her hair. Obviously, she...

□ a) likes to keep her hair very clean.

□ b) is playing hard to get.

□ c) isn't bright enough to come up with a new excuse.

□ d) has you confused with someone else.

4. A good-looking guy at the bar notices you and starts walking in your direction. As he approaches you, he trips on his own two feet and falls face first into your Tequila Sunrise. You should...

□ a) be proud that you saved his life by placing the drink in his way to break the fall.

□ b) ask him to buy you another drink.

□ c) tell him you prefer an orange slice to his nose in your drink.

□ d) offer him a straw.

5. You arrive at your blind date's house and your date, who answers the door, looks like she buys her clothes from Omar the Tent Maker. You should...

□ a) tell her you are a singing telegram and proceed to sing "Happy Birthday."

□ b) tell her you are looking to rent a similar apartment in the building and would like to measure the windows for curtains.

□ c) ask her if you can take her roommate out instead.

☐ d) order in pizza so none of your friends see you with her.

6. You are in a supermarket in the produce section and an interesting looking person is standing nearby. You should...
   ☐ a) take your shopping cart and ram it into that person.
   ☐ b) pick up a plastic lemon and ask the potential date if it's fresh.
   ☐ c) ask what a kiwi is.

7. Your friend gave you a name for a blind date and it was a disaster. You should...
   ☐ a) ask your friend for another name.
   ☐ b) go out with the date again just to be sure.
   ☐ c) ask your friend where she acquired her taste.
   ☐ d) call the IRS hot line and tell them your friend didn't report her racing winnings for the past 7 years.

8. You are on the beach sitting near a gorgeous blond and a guy who could play center for the Miami Dolphins walks over and kicks sand in your face. You should...
   ☐ a) thank him for bringing over some of his sand to share with you.
   ☐ b) dare him to do it again.
   ☐ c) move to another beach.
   ☐ d) ask the blond to defend your honor.

9. You stop at a red light in your '76 Nova and a handsome man in the Porsche next to you gives you a wink. You should...
   ☐ a) ask him if he wants to drag.
   ☐ b) tell him your Mercedes is in the shop right now.

□ c) "lip synch" that favorite tune on your radio and show him that MTV experience.

□ d) see if he will play bumper cars.

10. You take your date to a restaurant with the following menu and you only have $30 in your wallet:

ENTRE's		APPETIZERS	
Pheasant under glass	$22.50	Fruit cup	$ 4.50
Steak tartar	$18.00	Shrimp cocktail	$ 7.00
Alaskan King Crab	$25.00	Caesar salad(for 2)	$14.00
Chopped sirloin	$ 6.00		

DESSERTS

Coffee, tea	$5.75
Hot water	$2.00
Cheesecake	$4.00

You should...

□ a) explain the situation and beg your date to show some restraint.

□ b) enjoy your fruit cup slowly, as it will have to last you all evening.

□ c) plan on stiffing the waiter, maitre d', wine steward, and valet parking attendant.

□ d) assume your date will not order the Alaskan King Crab, shrimp cocktail, Caesar salad, cheesecake, and coffee and go ahead and order yourself the pheasant.

SCORING: Give yourself points as follows for each answer you chose (If you scored over 100 points, you obviously cheated...shame on you):

1.	(a) 2	(b) 1	(c) 3	(d) 4
2.	(a) 2	(b) 1	(c) 3	
3.	(a) 2	(b) 1	(c) 3	(d) 4
4.	(a) 3	(b) 2	(c) 4	(d) 1
5.	(a) 2	(b) 1	(c) 4	(d) 3
6.	(a) 1	(b) 2	(c) 3*	
7.	(a) 1	(b) 3	(c) 2	(d) 4
8.	(a) 4	(b) 3	(c) 1	(d) 2
9.	(a) 1	(b) 3	(c) 4	(d) 2
10.	(a) 1	(b) 4	(c) 3	(d) 2

*If you know what a kiwi is, give yourself an extra point.

If you scored between...

10–15   Do you even know what a date is?

16–30   No fair—You've dated before, haven't you?

31–38   You are obviously very good at multiple choice tests. Where were you when I was taking the law boards?

Show your friends how smart you are. Buy lots of copies of this book and let them compare their scores with yours.

What Is a Blind Date?

Chapter 3
Reasons for the Blind Date

"Oh No! I'm not getting stuck with the doofy-looking one."

Alternatives to the Blind Date

You are probably asking yourself why you should go on a blind date when there are so many wonderful alternatives, such as:

Singles Bars   • Ever try to pick up a woman in a group of twenty?

Health Clubs   • Can you compete with guys who look like Rambo?

Laundromats	• How many people clean their clothes more than once every six weeks?
Museums	• It's hard to meet someone in a place you have to whisper softer than at a golf tournament.
Your Office	• It's bad enough you have to be around these people 8 hours a day.
Supermarkets	• You could get hypothermia standing around the frozen food section all day.
Adult Education Courses	• You didn't go to classes in college. What makes you think you will start now?
Single-Oriented Vacations	• The only people who go are couples.

Now let's take a look at these alternatives in more detail:

Singles Bars

You are in this week's hottest night spot with a friend, looking to meet someone new. Your friend spots an attractive woman across the bar and points her out to you. He then recommends you go over there and meet her. (He has no intention of risking rejection himself.)

So, about ten minutes and six beers later you get up the nerve to go over there. Now you don't mind walking all the way across the bar. And getting rejected doesn't bother you...too much. What you really hate is that long walk back across the bar to your friend after she has told you she would rather spend the evening in the ladies room than talk to you.

But you do it anyway. You start walking and as you approach her, she sees you coming. She whispers something to her friend and they both laugh as you get closer. The pressure is mounting. You know your friend is watching this whole scene. "Hi! I was admiring your beautiful eyes and just had to come over to meet you. My name is Alan," you say. "That's nice," she responds and then turns back to chat with her friend. Since you have already committed yourself, you add, "What's your name?" "Dawn," she responds and again turns to finish her conversation with her friend about what color dress she looks best in.

Just as you turn around and start to walk away, another guy approaches Dawn and says, "Hi! I was admiring your beautiful eyes and just had to come over to meet you. My name is Bert." By the time you return to your friend, Dawn and Bert are already deciding whose apartment to go to for the rest of the evening.

Health Clubs

So you've joined a health club in your neighborhood. To do so you had to sign up for three years at an annual cost of $875 plus two years of indentured slavery. But that's only $2.39 a day, which is worth it since you "love" to exercise. Who can resist jogging in a circle 40 times around a 1/20th of a mile track to burn off 17 calories? Or jumping up and down while flapping your arms like a chicken to the sound of Tina Turner in an aerobics class?

Let's assume for a moment that your <u>sole</u> reason for joining the club was because you really do enjoy sweating after work and then putting your suit or dress back on so you can take it to the dry cleaners the next day. One day, however, it does occur to you that this place is a single's haven (of course, when you joined, this was the farthest thing from your mind). So you decide you are going to meet someone.

To get up your nerve, you decide to first take a relaxing sauna and shower. You need to make sure that whatever you do to meet someone, you do not embarrass yourself. Otherwise, you will have to face them every time you go to your health club. So a good, hot, relaxing sauna should soothe your nerves and clean your mind.

You go into the locker room, get undressed and walk into the sauna. As the door closes behind you, you realize you are in the co-ed sauna...and are the only one without any clothes on. Good work!

Laundromats

The trouble with laundromats is that corporate America has destroyed their potential as a place for meeting people by creating unrealistic expectations. You see, companies like Proctor & Gamble produce all those laundry detergents. So in order to sell them, they have big advertising agencies produce commercials showing how couples meet each other while "sharing a washing machine." Has that <u>ever</u> happened to you? Did anyone ever try to strike up a conversation with you in a laundromat by saying you had "ring around the collar?" If you were to even glance at a woman's underwear (I'm referring to her laundry), she'd think you were a sex fiend.

Museums

Depending on your choice of museum, this can be a very productive place for meeting someone. Science museums, natural history museums, and any place with Walt Disney characters are definitely out, since they attract single parents and family outings. You are best to stick with art museums—but nothing too esoteric.

So you decide to go to the Museum of Modern Art on a Tuesday night to get a little culture and possibly meet someone new. After spending an hour viewing paintings that look like AAA road maps and sculptures similar to the ones you create with your own trash compactor, you are about to give up.

But alas, your efforts were not in vain! Across the room past a class of school children and over by the hub cap exhibit, you spot someone you would like to meet. You casually make your way through the crowd of munchkins to approach him and make some witty remark, which he loves (one of those rare occasions when a quality "opener" actually came to you).

You hit it off at once and make plans to have dinner together on Saturday night. You say your goodbyes and head for the museum exit. Over your shoulder you hear your new friend say "Come on kids; time to go." As you turn around to look, eleven kids respond "Yes, DAD!" It appears he not only forgot to mention his kids, but also that he has enough for a football team.

Your Office

Now everyone will tell you never date someone at work. And there is a very good reason for it. If things go sour, it could be very uncomfortable for the both of you to see each other day-in and day-out.

But, there is also a positive side to this. Your significant other may get promoted to president of the company and your career could be set for life, assuming your relationship continues to go well. If not, well, that's what executive search firms are for.

So, don't totally discount your office as a place to meet someone. You are exposed to a large number of people you might not normally get the chance to meet. The successful ones will probably already be married, but success is not the most important quality to look for anyway (is it?)

One day you go into the marketing department to discuss the budget on a new promotional campaign with someone named Ms. Washburn. You walk into her office only to meet a very attractive and intelligent woman with a bare ring finger on her left hand. (We will assume for the moment that she is single.)

Push comes to shove and you start dating each other. After three months you become less discreet at the office about your relationship. And so it becomes common knowledge that you and Ms. Washburn are an "item." You are very content and on top of the world. Your newfound relationship has put you in a better framework, which has had a positive effect on your work. What more could you ask for?

A promotion. Your boss Tom Geteven calls you into his office to tell you that you have been promoted and will be getting a 40% salary increase. Congratulations! You have just been promoted to Director of Indian operations and will have to relocate to Bangladesh immediately. It seems that <u>Ms.</u> Washburn used to be <u>Mrs.</u> Geteven before she divorced Tom. So much for office romance.

Supermarkets

The fruit and vegetable section of the supermarket is probably one of the last open frontiers of dating. It was actually designed specifically to facilitate meeting people, as opposed to purchasing the evening's side dishes.

Feigning ignorance on how to tell if a piece of fruit is ripe or not is the technique most commonly employed to strike up a conversation with someone in a supermarket. You simply have to stand with a confused look on your face, while holding a piece of cantaloupe in one hand. When someone you would like to meet passes by, just stop them and ask for their advice on your fruit. (It is not proper to offer to check her melons...at least not in public.)

This technique, while still very effective, has lost its appeal over the years due to the increased assortment of frozen fruit and vegetable dishes. You must adjust your approach slightly: Stand in the frozen foods section with a box of frozen vegetables in your hand and the same confused look as before. When you stop someone, ask if one of the chemical ingredients, oxycilic acid, will make you sterile. If the person responds with "Who cares?", try the dairy department.

Adult Education

There is a wide variety of adult education classes you can take beyond the conversational French given at your local high school. There are now courses on everything from white water rafting to how to lose your foreign accent. Most of the people who take these classes are single, so this would appear to be a great way to learn something new and also meet someone.

So you sign up for "Dirty Dancing," a one-hour class teaching all forty-six dance steps from the movie. Like most men, you know the basic box step, which you use only at weddings and bar mitzvahs. With popular music you just shuffle your feet back and forth, looking like you just drank four cups of coffee and are waiting on line for the men's room.

But you figure it is about time you learned how to dance properly, and who knows, maybe you will meet someone nice. When the class begins, the instructor pairs you up with someone who isn't nearly as experienced on the dance floor as you are. But that's okay—at least you won't look foolish.

After 45 minutes of dance lessons, which included 44 minutes of stepping on your partner's feet, the lesson ends. You can now practice your newfound skills on anyone in the class for the last 15 minutes. Finally, the moment of truth.

You see "her" standing across the room. She glances at you and then looks away. You glance back. She is exquisite. Her feet are tapping in perfect rhythm with the music, just waiting for someone to dance with. You "glide" across the dance studio with your feet barely touching the floor.

"Yes!" She would love to dance with you. This is your big moment. Forty-five long and grueling minutes of intensive lessons are under your belt and you are not about to let them go to waste. She has been dancing for eleven years, but that doesn't intimidate you in the least.

The two of you start to dance in perfect harmony (well, almost). For her it is effortless. For you it is 15 minutes of deep concentration broken only by beads of sweat pouring down your forehead. Why aren't those feet doing what you told them to do? They seemed to know what to do during the lessons.

Fortunately, she doesn't appear to notice your "novel" style of dancing...until you spin her.

Now nobody said anything about not spinning someone near a wall. Nor did they happen to mention anything about "catching her." How were you supposed to know that she just had her nose done?

Single-Oriented Vacations

Your travel agent just handed you your airline tickets to Club Sex, "the Caribbean vacation where everybody gets lucky!" The travel brochure shows pictures of attractive men and women on deserted beaches at sunset with wild orgies everywhere. Sounds great, doesn't it?

The concept looks great, so you book a trip and go down to the island of Aruba. When you arrive down there, you realize a problem right off the bat: There are 678 women at the resort and only 673 men. That means that if everyone pairs off, five females will be alone.

The pressure mounts. What if you are one of the five? You scout around looking for five useless women who could not possibly get a man interested in them. That would solve the problem (not for them, of course). There is one over by the roller skate rental booth. Another with seven pens and a pocket liner in her shirt pocket. Then three more. You are safe. The pressure is off...until dinner time when two men had to be flown off the island due to food poisoning. Luckily, you meet a man after dinner and wonder who the poor soul was who would be spending the week by herself.

How Desperate Are You?

Let's face facts. If your social life was that great, you wouldn't even be reading this book. You are obviously not in the middle of a serious relationship or dating a dozen different people (unless, of course, blind dating is how you are able to date so many).

Therefore, you are most likely in what I like to call the *desperate* category. There is nothing wrong with this. You are probably just ending a relationship or have just moved into a new town. If not, have you considered using a different deodorant?

You know you're desperate when...

> ...you take a week-long vacation and there are no messages on your answering machine.

> ...you bought a two-seater sports car and no one has ever sat in the passenger seat.

> ...you never make use of the two-for-one specials at the local movie theater.

...you go through your mail on Valentine's Day and it is all addressed to "occupant."

...you have spent the last five New Year's Eves drinking ginger ale and watching your kitchen TV as the ball drops.

...you continuously call the operator to make sure your phone still rings.

...you eat "soup for one" with Dan Rather every night.

...you bought a king-size bed, but you sleep on your couch.

...you win a trip for two to the French Riviera, but turn it down and take the toaster oven instead.

...you buy a picture frame and decide to keep the picture that came with it.

...you write a book on blind dating to get dates.

SECTION II:

How to Get Names

Chapter 4
The Normal Method

"Trust me. She's got a great personality."

Whom to Ask for Names

The first step in getting a blind date is the name; it's hard to start without one. Married friends are the best source for names because they feel it is a sin that everyone isn't married. In technical terms, anyone who gives you a name is called a blind date broker. This person is not necessarily a professional, unless the initials P.B.D.B. (Professional Blind Date Broker) appear after the name. (See sample Federal licensing exam at end of this section.)

Friends who are moving out of town are another reliable source. Ask your friends for the names and phone numbers of all the people they dated.

Acquiring names is not as haphazard a process as one might suspect. You are not limited to immediate friends and relatives of people you know. Simply think of yourself as a product to be marketed (I threw this in to appeal to the MBA audience). First, set your goals and objectives (i.e. what type of person you are looking for). Then choose a "sales force" to help you. Comprise your sales force of your own friends and married friends of your parents who have stopped thinking of you as the kid who spilled grape juice on their oriental rug.

Your parents' friends will not find you dates unless they know you want to be fixed up. I personally have a "sales force" enlisted of a dozen couples, all friends of my parents. When any of them meets an unattached woman in my age group, they give me her name. I have one friend of my parents who actually approaches women she does not know, introduces herself, and asks if that woman would mind meeting me.

Now consider media and promotional strategies. That's right—you can't expect a sales force alone to do all the work. A media strategy should include a mix of personal ads (see chapter 7) in various newspapers and magazines. The promotional strategy should include a sweepstakes program and some cross promotions.

The Professional Blind Date Broker Exam

In order to be licensed as a P.B.D.B., an applicant must fulfill the following requirements:

{1} The applicant must pass the Professional Blind Date Broker Exam, given annually on Valentine's Day in one of those hotels in the Poconos with heart-shaped swimming pools.

{2} The applicant must have coordinated a minimum of ten blind dates within the past year. These dates must be documented and filed in the appropriate states in the county clerk's office.

{3} The applicant must be over the age of 18.

{4} The applicant must not wear loud clothing, drive purple Cadillacs, or collect money for arranging dates. (See section 450.2-58 of the Federal regulations re: Professional Pimp Exam).

Sample Questions:

1. A Yenta is...
   - ☐ a) a matchmaker.
   - ☐ b) a blind date broker.
   - ☐ c) a pain in the ass.
   - ☐ d) all of the above.

2. A fix up is...
   - ☐ a) a method of torture devised by Vincent Price.
   - ☐ b) taking drugs on an airplane.
   - ☐ c) what the mechanic does to your car after you smash into your garage door.
   - ☐ d) a blind date.

3. You are asked to find a companion for a man who is loud, obnoxious, conceited, boring, and rich. The perfect person for him should be...
   - ☐ a) loud, obnoxious, conceited, and boring.
   - ☐ b) quiet, soft-spoken, modest, and interesting.
   - ☐ c) deaf with a talent for spending money.
   - ☐ d) any woman with a pulse.

4. You are asked to find a companion for a woman who is very attractive, intelligent, warm, giving, and very successful. The perfect person for her should be...
   - ☐ a) handsome, intelligent, warm, giving, and very successful.
   - ☐ b) ugly, stupid, insensitive, selfish, and a bum.
   - ☐ c) the author of this book.
   - ☐ d) any man with a pulse.

5. You are married to a wonderful man and have a sister who is 37 and still single. You meet a 40-year-old real estate executive who could be a Paul Newman look-alike. He is divorced with no children and interested in meeting someone new. You should...
   - ☐ a) introduce him to your sister.
   - ☐ b) introduce him to one of your single friends for whom you are also actively looking to find a companion.
   - ☐ c) do nothing.
   - ☐ d) divorce your husband and ask "Paul" out for a drink.

SCORING: Give yourself points as follows for each answer you chose:

1.   (a) 1   (b) 1   (c) 1   (d) 3

2.	(a) 3		(b) 0		(c) 1		(d) 2
3.	(a) 1		(b) 0		(c) 3		(d) 2
4.	(a) 1		(b) 0		(c) 3		(d) 2
5.	(a) 1		(b) 1		(c) 0		(d) 3

If you scored between...

0– 5   You would have been a great help to Noah matching pairs for his ark.

6–10   Four out of five of your "matches" will end up in marriage...and then divorce.

11–15   You were born with the gift of matchmaking.

Whom Not to Ask for Names

Never take names from single friends who would not date the people they are willing to fix you up with— if the person is so great, why is your friend so willing to give you the name? Other potential matchmakers to forget are: grandparents, your mother, clergy, mailmen, and your boss.

Let's look at why some of these people are poor choices ...

Clergy

Clergymen are poor choices because they see only the good in people. Their single criteria for a match is that the two parties be of the same faith. I once found myself in a small Southern town, where the singles population was surpassed only by the number of all-night discos. Just to meet someone new, I drove 230 miles to the nearest large city and looked for a rabbi to help me.

After finding one and telling him my plight, he offered me the name and phone number of a young lady named Karen. I called her that evening. We chatted awhile and I told her the rabbi had given me her name.

JEFF: Listen, why don't we get together sometime?

KAREN: Sure. I would love to.

JEFF: How about dinner on Thursday? I could pick you up at your house around 7.

KAREN: Sounds great. I'll see you then.

JEFF: Wait! By the way, what is your last name?

KAREN: Dinkerhoffer.

JEFF: What a coincidence; Rabbi Dinkerhoffer gave me your name.

KAREN: What a coincidence; Rabbi Dinkerhoffer is my father.

Grandparents

As a general rule, grandparents do not have discerning tastes when it comes to your future mate. They want great-grandchildren and will stop at nothing to achieve this goal. Every grandmother has at least one doctor or lawyer up her sleeve, accompanied by the refrain "you could do worse." (...and you have.)

For years, I'm sure, you avoided your grandparents' attempts to fix you up with someone. You suffered the guilt of comments like, "We just want you to be happy," implying you could never be happy as a single person. And, of course, the classic— "We're not trying to rush you into getting married...it's just that we won't be around forever, you know."

Well, one time my grandmother went so far as to borrow a photograph of the prospective date to show me. Much to my surprise the woman was gorgeous. When I asked my grandmother where this treasure lived, she told me the address was on the back of the photo (someone was really prepared). She lived in Durham, North Carolina, 1200 miles from where I lived. "How could you even consider fixing me up with this woman? She lives in North Carolina," I yelled. "What, airplanes don't fly there?", she replied with a smug look.

Incentive Programs

Many companies set up incentive systems to motivate their sales forces to sell more products. Using the same concept, you can set up a sweepstakes program and cross promotions to meet people.

Sweepstakes Programs

The key to any sweepstakes program is to properly communicate it to your "sales force." Explain your program to those people who could potentially give you names and phone numbers. Don't forget to include past dates who might have cute friends for you. This just goes to show that each and every date, no matter how ugly or boring, is worthwhile. (There are exceptions, of course—someone named "Mongo" could not possibly know anyone you would ever consider dating.)

To begin, develop a point system that will enable people to earn valuable prizes. For example, everyone who gets at least 11 points will receive a free bottle of cologne or perfume. At the end of three months, everyone who was in the above category would be eligible for the drawing of a grand prize, such as a Ferrari or Porsche (the prize has to be big enough to warrant their efforts, so forget the Ginsu knives).

To obtain points, people simply have to fix you up with someone. For every person you are fixed up with, the blind date broker receives one point. To encourage quality over quantity the broker will receive three additional points if you have more than one date with the same person. Thus, it only takes three quality names and phone numbers (or eleven duds) to be eligible for valuable prizes. See how easy it is?!

Cross Promotions

This concept originated from the major consumer goods companies. A coupon is usually included with a product for a discount on other products. This is done to get people to try other products from the same manufacturer.

You can modify this promotional idea to help you get new names. The key is to get a couple of your single friends who are also interested in blind dating. When one of you goes on a date that does not turn out well, that person then gives the date's name and phone number to one of the other members of your group. For this to work properly, it is important that only valid names be passed along. Any dates with a family tree linked to Lizzie Borden or Charles Manson should be excluded.

Pre-Date Research

Whenever possible, try to find out from the broker as much as you can about your potential blind date, such as:

> literacy
>
> credit history
>
> parents' estimated net worth
>
> car make and model
>
> any prior convictions
>
> salary potential
>
> photographs

Sources for this information can include: Dun & Bradstreet, FBI reports, friends, neighbors, co-workers, and the local bank president.

On the next page is a sample form that the person arranging the blind date should fill out in advance:

Cues and Clues

By now, you have gathered some vital information about a prospective blind date. It is important to analyze that information to determine if there is something about this person which should clue you not to call. Areas to watch out for are job types, college background (if any), sports interests, and community involvement.

Blind Date Application Form

NAME:_____
          first   last (if known)

NICKNAME:_____
          (if Buffy, Biff, Rin Tin Tin, or Motorcycle
          Mama, do not bother filling out rest of form)

PHONE:(___**)**   -_____   (800)_____-_____

PLACE OF RESIDENCE:
- ☐ Parents' home
- ☐ Own home
- ☐ Friends/lovers

TYPE OF RESIDENCE:
- ☐ Mansion   ☐ House
- ☐ Ten-story walk-up   ☐ Park bench

AGE:
- ☐ Younger than your niece
- ☐ Just right
- ☐ Has children your age

MARITAL STATUS:
- ☐ Single
- ☐ Single, wishes s/he was married
- ☐ Married
- ☐ Married, wishes s/he was single
- ☐ Divorced
- ☐ Not sure

EX-GIRLFRIENDS:
- ☐ Intelligent, sexy and fun
- ☐ Sexy, fun and intelligent
- ☐ Fun, intelligent and sexy
- ☐ He hasn't had a date in seven years

EX-BOYFRIENDS:
- ☐ Big
- ☐ Very big
- ☐ Very big with a bad temper
- ☐ Very big and jealous with a bad temper
- ☐ She hasn't had a date in seven years

EDUCATION (if any):
Highest Grade Completed
- ☐ Kindergarten
- ☐ High School
- ☐ College
- ☐ Stanford Law School
- ☐ Divinity Training
- ☐ School of Cosmetology, Air Conditioning, & Auto Repair

OCCUPATION:
- ☐ Physician
- ☐ Accountant
- ☐ Computer Programmer
- ☐ Garbage Collector
- ☐ Member of Congress
- ☐ President of AT&T
- ☐ Other_____
- ☐ None (Doesn't understand the meaning of the word "work"

WORK HOURS:
- ☐ 9-5
- ☐ Graveyard shift
- ☐ Whenever convenient to get out of a date

PRINCIPAL SOURCE OF INCOME:
- ☐ Work
- ☐ Clips T-bill coupons
- ☐ Clips food stamp coupons
- ☐ Is waiting to win the Publishers' Clearing House Sweepstakes

CREDIT CARDS OWNED:
- ☐ Visa/MasterCard
- ☐ American Express (☐ green ☐ gold ☐ platinum)
- ☐ None (prefers shoplifting)

PRINCIPAL MEANS OF TRANSPORTATION:
- ☐ Porsche
- ☐ Bicycle
- ☐ '79 Pinto
- ☐ Reeboks

HEIGHT:
- ☐ Needs a highchair at dinner in a restaurant
- ☐ Average
- ☐ Can go apple picking without a ladder

WEIGHT:
- ☐ Anorexic
- ☐ Average
- ☐ Could lose 100 pounds and no one could tell the difference

LOOKS (describing potential female dates):
- ☐ Often confused with Christy Brinkley's better-looking sister
- ☐ Often mistaken for that famous actress, Lassie
- ☐ She has a great personality

LOOKS (describing potential male dates):
- ☐ Often confused with Robert Redford's better-looking brother
- ☐ Often mistaken for that famous actor, Alf
- ☐ He has a great personality

HOBBIES:
- ☐ Hotel towel collecting
- ☐ Rock collecting
- ☐ Chasing cars
- ☐ Reading Dr. Seuss books

SPORTS:
- ☐ Tennis
- ☐ Jogging
- ☐ Skiing
- ☐ Tetherball
- ☐ Shopping
- ☐ Roller Derby
- ☐ Mud Wrestling
- ☐ Exercise is a four-letter word

BELIEFS:
- ☐ Astrology
- ☐ ESP
- ☐ Tooth Fairy
- ☐ Was once abducted by a UFO

COMMON CAUSES:
- ☐ Political campaigns
- ☐ Environmental organizations
- ☐ "Save the Whales"
- ☐ "Save the red M&Ms"

College

Let's say she went to college. Which one did she attend? There is a big gap between Harvard and Ralph's Refrigerator Maintenance School. In essence, you want someone with an education level similar to yours. For example, you studied at M.I.T. for four years, barely seeing anything besides the inside of the engineering library and your dorm room. A friend gives you the phone number of a woman named Trish who was on the six-year plan at the University of Miami.

Trish would have graduated earlier, but she spent too much time partying with her professors to go to class. Face facts: You will bore her to death. Your idea of fun is discussing Carl Sagan topics, not hitting the beach to "catch a few rays."

Careers

For the most part it really doesn't matter what your date's career is, but you do have to be careful. If, for example, she is like most people, she spends between 40 and 60 hours per week at her job, not including the extra 15 hours per week deciding what to wear to work. On the other hand, you only have to decide which of your four ties goes best with the suit.

Since his job encompasses so much time of his life (as does yours), you can expect your conversations will occasionally center around his career. The major difference is that he actually thinks his career is important. Just remember this next time you date a bookkeeper.

Psychologist

Most people would consider psychology a perfectly respectable profession, which it is. But dating people who chose it is not always easy. Maybe it's me, but on a first date I personally don't like being asked questions like "Were you toilet trained at a very young age?" (On a second date, however, I am willing to discuss how my inability to find inner peace relates back to when I failed finger painting in kindergarten.)

Clothing buyer

Let's say she's a clothing buyer for Macy's department stores. Her job is to travel around the world and purchase clothing for the chain of stores. In essence, she is a "professional" shopper; she shops for a living! We are not talking about an amateur here. We are talking about a full fledged professional. The amateur has no chance whatsoever of spending money nearly as fast as the professional. She carries more credit on her charge cards than most Third World countries. You'd have to take a second mortgage just to get past the first date.

Lawyer

Lawyers can also be tough, but it really depends on what kind. If he earns his living chasing ambulances, he will sue anything in sight. (His sister is still paying damages for biting him in sixth grade.) But despite the hazards, you decide to go out with him anyway. During your initial phone conversation, you make some reference to the fact that you both will have a great time. He accepts this as an oral contract. The date turns out lousy and you wake up the next morning with a subpoena instead of him. On the other hand, had things worked out, he could have fixed your parking tickets for life.

Nuns & Priests

Nuns and priests don't go on blind dates.

School teacher

In the old days there were much higher standards for hiring teachers than there are today. So you can't rely on the Board of Education as a screening process anymore. You can easily tell a school teacher from your pre-date phone call. Out of habit a teacher will use phrases like "Pay attention!" "How many times do I have to tell you that?!" "Keep your voice down...I can hear you." Could dinner with this date be much better?

Veterinarian

You could do worse. To be a veterinarian she must be intelligent, have a love for animals, and be financially secure (you know...rich). However, her parents might have pushed her to become a veterinarian because there was no way in the world she'd ever find someone to support her.

Another thing to be aware of is that a veterinarian has a built-in method of ending a blind date quickly. At any time after she meets you, she simply has to trigger her beeper and excuse herself to call her answering service. When she returns, she will tell you she has to leave for an emergency operation—a horse needs stitches in its rump. No, she does not mind spending a few hours with another horse's ass.

Community Involvement

Another thing to screen for is how well-known your date is in the community. If he has a wide circle of friends, you are probably better off giving the name and number to someone you don't like. Otherwise, he might blacklist you from getting dates with people he knows.

Suppose you decide to ask a man (we'll call Jim) out. After a few dates you realize that he is somewhat less than the man of your dreams and you decide to stop seeing him. Well, Jim gets angry and tells all his friends what a louse you are. And to make sure he doesn't leave anyone out, he sends a letter to everyone he knows, making up stories about you so you will be blacklisted:

Dear friend,

As you may or may not know, I dated <u>Linda</u> a few times and we recently stopped seeing each other.

While you, of course, can do what you want, I would strongly recommend you <u>don't ever go out with her</u>. She is loud, obnoxious, boring, cheap, selfish, inconsiderate, rude, demeaning, ignorant, pushy, unambitious, temperamental, and stupid. And those are just a few of her good qualities.

Please pass this letter along to someone else you know so we can make sure Linda never has a date again!

Yours truly,

Jim

P.S. Don't forget to add Linda's name to the list of others I sent you this past month:

Allison	Lisa
Alana	Mara
Stacey	Lauren

Sports Activities

While sports activity really is not an issue of whether or not to call a particular blind date, there are one or two to watch out for. My father always told me, "Never date a girl bigger than you because you could get hurt."

For example, you go out with a very petite woman who is a superb conversationalist. As the evening progresses and the drinks flow, you get into an amorous mood and make a pass at her (or rather a fumble). As you reach your arms around to embrace her, she grabs your right arm, kicks your left leg out from under you and throws you to the ground. It is in the hospital the next day when she tells you she is a brown belt in judo. (Now you lead with your left arm, per doctor's orders.)

Geographical Undesirables

In this age of world travel you must also look out for G.U.s (Geographical Undesirables) and avoid them like the plague. A G.U. is a potential date who does not live within commuting distance of your home. Blind dating is difficult enough as it is without having to add 3,000 miles to it.

If you live in St. Louis, someone from Atlanta would be considered a G.U. If you live in Boston, someone from Detroit would be considered a G.U. If you live in Nome, Alaska, everyone is considered a G.U. A simple rule of thumb is that your blind date should not live more than a thumb's distance on your local map. (Do not use an 8-1/2 x 11 inch map of the United States for this or your next blind date could be with someone in Bolivia.)

In the business world you could meet someone who is just in town for the day and flying back across the country that evening. It's tough to convince your boss to send you to Ft. Lauderdale "on business" just to see someone you met at lunch (with the right patter, however, this can be accomplished with minimal risk of losing your job. I managed to have my boss send me there so I could spend a week with a woman who was going to be in Ft. Lauderdale for vacation. Naturally, once I was able to get my boss to commit to it, the woman changed her plans and I never heard from her again).

Anyone living overseas would normally be considered a G.U., but there are exceptions. Last year while I was in London overnight for business, I visited my cousin Kate and her husband John who live there. In an effort to promote international blind dating, they arranged a dinner date for me for that evening.

My cousins and I went to a seafood restaurant and my date was going to meet us there. Kate told me the name of my blind date for the evening, which sounded very familiar. When she showed up, I recognized her as a blind date I had three years prior back home in New York. She, however, didn't remember ever meeting me. Since she actually lives in New York, she would not be considered a Geographical Undesirable. However, since I made such a *wonderful* impression on her the first time, in that she would not want to go out with me again, we will leave her in the G.U. category.

Chapter 5

Dating Services

"I think I have just the person for you..."

You've tried everything else and nothing seems to work. You have met quite a few people and have had a number of blind dates, but still haven't met the person of your dreams. Maybe it's time you tried a more structured approach to the blind dating game—dating services.

Dating services have changed over the years and now take on many forms. They can be broken down into four categories: (1) computer dating, (2) personalized matching, (3) video dating, and (4) auto dating. The former two match you up, while the latter two let you choose your own potential date. The first types are the

---

most common and usually keep in the key aspect of blind dating—the blind date broker.

Advertising for dating services all looks very similar. Usually they consist of a picture of a happy couple with captions underneath such as "Are you tired of singles bars?" There are a few ads which are more direct, like the Last Chance Dating Service: "Have you been rejected by other dating services? We'll find you someone even if we have to comb every alley and sewer in the city."

In any event, you see an ad that catches your eye and you call the company for information. Three days later an envelope arrives at your home with the return address of "Can't Get a Date Dating Service." Inside is a letter describing the wonderful dates the company will supply you with, including the promise of some imaginary number of matches they will make for you each month. Any service promising you over 31 matches per month should be viewed with some skepticism, especially in February.

The service will offer a variety of different membership plans ranging anywhere from one month to seven years (for the terminally undatable). Some will even guarantee that one of your matches will end up in marriage. These dating services are able to offer such guarantees by using illegal aliens for most of their matches.

After you decide which membership plan you want, you must then fill out an application form, which makes your last loan request look pale in comparison. There are questions on everything from your shoe size to your eyesight (this helps them decide how good-looking your date has to be). Once this is completed, you are invited to come to the dating service's office for an interview with a counselor. The whole process is like applying for a job...for the position of someone's mate.

Computer Dating

If you cannot afford one with personalized service, you will be stuck with the computer dating service. (It is kind of like not being able to afford a lawyer and having a court appoint one for you). You fill out a form describing yourself and also the type of person you would like to date. This information is fed into a computer, which matches you up with someone who resembles your ex-husband. But then what did you expect for $49.95?

Personalized Matching

If you can afford $1,000 or more, you can get personalized introductions to other people who also shelled out that kind of money. Here at least you have a better chance of meeting someone who is financially secure—either that or someone who hocked her living room furniture to join this service.

The person who does the introductions usually looks like someone's Jewish mother. Instead of having you fill out a lengthy form, she will sit you down with a nice cup of tea and determine whether you meet one of the major eligibility criteria: "Are you a doctor? How about a lawyer? An accountant at least? No? Have you tried one of those computerized services?" When she is done quizzing you, she will go through her files and then fix you up with her daughter.

Video Dating

This is the kind of service in which you choose your own date. You make a five-minute video of yourself, which then goes into the company's video library. If being in front of a camera makes you nervous, an actor or actress will be supplied to stand in for you. Other people can look at your video at any time and you can look at theirs. If you both are interested, the service gives each of you the other's phone number.

This sort of takes all the fun out of blind dating. Since you already know what the other person looks like, you don't get the "joy" of wondering who will be meeting you at the restaurant. And before you even call him or her for the first time, you are given the complete biography. This information supplied by the dating service is more complete than that of a presidential candidate.

Auto Dating

Have you ever been driving along and seen someone you would like to meet in another car? You step on the gas to catch up to the other car, only to have have some little old lady going 30 MPH on the highway cut in front of you in the left lane. For the next ten miles you jockey for position until finally your car is on the other car's passenger side. You catch the driver's eye and smile. She smiles back. You then make that circular motion with your hand to signal her to roll down her passenger window (kind of like the motion of cranking up a Model T Ford).

She doesn't have power windows so she reaches across to the handle on the passenger's side, while holding the steering wheel in her left hand. As she does this, she accidentally pulls on the steering wheel, veering her car smack into yours, causing a six-car collision. Nice going! I'm sure she will want to meet you now...at least to get the name of your insurance company.

Auto dating services were designed to alleviate this problem. When you sign up for this service, you are given a bumper sticker with a number on it and stating that you are part of this service. When someone sees you driving, they can get your name and phone number through the service by the number on your bumper sticker. This probably would have saved you $2,700 in auto body work.

Chapter 6
Dating Game Shows

"Congratulations, Rhonda, for choosing bachelor number 3."

While dating game shows make up only a small percentage of all blind dates, they are worth mentioning. The major difficulty with this form of blind dating is that only a limited number of people can get on these shows. If you do manage to get on one, congratulations, now 80 million households across the country will know you have trouble getting a date.

Presently, there are two types of dating game shows: The kind where you get to ask your potential dates absurd questions without seeing them and the kind where you see them, but cannot ask any questions.

The Game with Questions

The best example of this is The Dating Game, which has been around for years. (Actually, now it is called The *All New* Dating Game, which means all the furniture got reupholstered, including the MC). This game works as follows: Three contestants sit on one side of a wall and answer questions provided by a person (we'll call the interrogator) sitting on the other side of the wall. These questions are designed to get a true understanding of what the contestants are really like: If we were on a sinking ship and I had the only life preserver, tell me why I should give it to you instead? What games can you develop with a food processor? If I was Snow White, which of the Seven Dwarfs would you be? (Sleazy was not one of the Dwarfs.)

After the interrogator asks these and similar thought- provoking questions for ten minutes, he or she gets to choose one of the three contestants (otherwise known as bachelors and bachelorettes) for a date. The winner, the interrogator, and a chaperone go for four days all expenses paid to some romantic destination like the Love Canal in Buffalo, NY. The runners-up get cancellation prizes like a six-month supply of Spam.

The Game without Questions

The best example of this is The Love Connection. This game works as follows: Three contestants make a thirty-second video of themselves talking about some important aspect of dating, like should the man sit on the right side or left side of his date in a movie theater. (We'll leave the answer to this inspiring question for the sequel to this book.)

The player, the person who gets to go out with one of the three charmers, talks about him or herself in person to the game show host. The audience then casts its vote electronically for the contestant they think the player would like the best. (Personally, I don't like the idea of some guy in the studio audience saying to himself, "I'm gonna pick the bacteriologist with no teeth and the toupee; that should make for a *real* fun date!") Then, to make the contestants feel good, the percentage of the audience that chose them is displayed next to their video picture.

The real fun comes when they bring the lucky couple back on the show after the date. There, on national television, they say what a lousy date they had, including the personal eating habits of their dates. Can you think of anything more enjoyable than having a studio audience critique your dating style?

I don't recommend either game show method as they will just give added joy to your last significant other who sees you on the show and now knows you can't get a date.

Chapter 7
The Personals

"Let me repeat the ad. Sexy blond 5' 6", slim model,..."

Why Use Personal Ads?

A personal ad is a form of blind date without the middleman (or blind date broker). Thus, there is no one to give you any references on the other person, which makes this form of blind date very risky.

Yet, the use of personal ads has grown dramatically over the past few years. This phenomenon has been fueled primarily by the increasing difficulty of single people to meet each other and the limited amount of free time we have to look. Many major magazines and newspapers now take personal ads, which turn out to

---

be more profitable for the publisher than a full-page advertisement for toilet bowl cleaner.

You know damn well anyone placing a personal ad is going to lie through his or her teeth...much like any other form of advertising except there is no organization to oversee it. Anyway, there are two ways to go about this: You can respond to personal ads or you can place your own ads. It is best to use a combination of the two.

Responding to Personal Ads

Responding to a personal ad has a major advantage over placing an ad: cost. For example, a 30-line ad (1080 characters) with box number placed in *New York* magazine would cost $840. Responding to that same ad would cost only 25¢ in postage. Therefore, you could respond to 3,360 personal ads before breaking even. In other words, the ad described would have to pull 3,360 responses to make it worthwhile. Get serious!

OK. You have decided to respond to a couple of ads. What is the first step? You must understand the abbreviations people use to limit the number of characters in the ad and thereby the cost. A list of the more popular ones is shown below:

B	Black	S	Single
J	Jewish	D	Divorced
C	Catholic	W	White
F	Female	P	Protestant
M	Male	G	Gay
H	Happy		

So, by combining a few letters, the author of an ad can save a number of words. For example, SBCM would stand for Single, Black, Catholic Male and DWJF would stand for Divorced, White, Jewish Female. Now you try supplying the abbreviation for White, Gay, Single Male:

— — — —

If you answered WGSM, you were correct.

Sometimes people use abbreviations that are a little less well-known. However, it is important to recognize these if you are going to respond to an ad so you do not make a terrible faux pas. Here are some lesser-known abbreviations:

A   Alimony recipient (not interested in remarrying and losing the support check)

E   Egghead

I   Illiterate

U   Undesirable

R   Rich

T   Teeny-bopper

Z   Zero

Now, using a combination of the familiar and unfamiliar codes, how would you abbreviate a Protestant, Undesirable, Teeny-bopper, who is a real Zero?

— — — —

Now that you have the hang of these abbreviations, let's take a look at some actual personal ads we found and analyze them. This will enable you to prescreen ads you might respond to. First, memorize the following rules:

RULE #1: Always respond to an ad that is over 40 lines long. (Anyone who can afford such an ad is probably very wealthy and worth contacting).

RULE #2: Never respond to an ad that does not ask for a photo or considers it optional. (If that person doesn't care what you look like, you probably don't want to see that person either.)

RULE #3: Always add 8 years to any woman who lists her age as either 29, 39, or 49; deduct 4 inches off any man's height; and add 10 pounds to both genders' weight.

RULE #4: Never put your return address on the envelope, unless it is a post office box. (You don't want some slimebucket dropping in on your front doorstep at 2 in the morning.)

RULE #5: Always subtract at least half of the assets listed in the ad. (Men, especially, have a slight tendency to exaggerate their wealth—among other things.)

RULE #6: Never respond to an ad written by someone's mother:

> "JEWISH mother looking for a cute SJF with a nice personality 22-28 for SJM son 28 who is good looking, witty, intelligent, creative and a mensch."

Take a look at the analysis of these two ads:

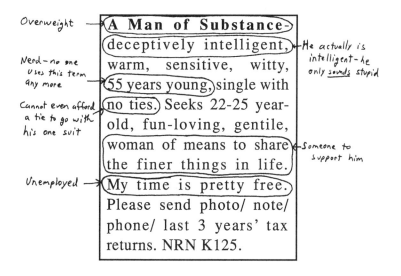

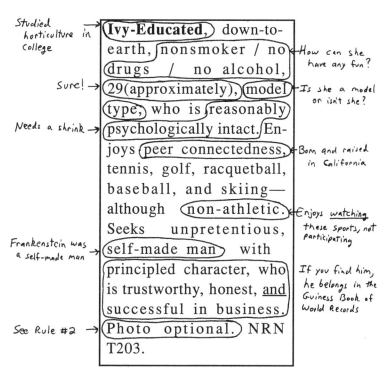

Now that you understand all of the rules, take the following quiz. For each pair of personal ads, choose the one to which you would be more likely to respond.

1. ☐ A. STRIKINGLY PRETTY MD - 32, 5'7", slim, softly feminine, sensual, sincere, affectionate, giving. Enjoys swimming, biking, art, theater, classical music, and long walks. Seeks insightful, intelligent, accomplished man 30-42, with strength of soul and character. Phone/note/photo. LAT N115.

   ☐ B. RECENTLY DIVORCED HOUSEWIFE - 39, with 9 children under 14, presentable and socially acceptable. Enjoys reading, TV, and walking my dogs (3 Doberman Pincers). Looking for fatherly type with a good face and large house. No photos please. SD PT109.

2. ☐ A. MULTIMILLIONAIRE - I own my own business with sales in the millions, but have no one to share the profits with. 35 and a Yale graduate, I enjoy weekend trips by private jet to my chateau in Monte Carlo and ballooning over the Swiss Alps. If you are 24-37, loving, intelligent, and not money-oriented, let's meet at one of my condos in NY,CA,MA,IL,TX,CO. Send note/photo. TEX R99.

   ☐ B. MALE, MINT CONDITION - Only one previous owner. 38 years of good performance with only minor maintenance. Clean, shiny top, slightly-worn seat. If you enjoy long drives in the country with your top down and drive-in movies, grab your polish and send photo/phone/note. RT214.

KEY: If you chose "B" for either question, go back and reread the previous sections. If you chose "A" for question one and know someone who fits that description, please send her name and phone number to Jeff Nagel, c/o Blind Date Research, Blockbuster Publications, Inc.

Now that you have mastered the art of analyzing personal ads, you need to learn how to write a proper letter of response. Oh yes! This is not something you do to pass the time while you sit on the john. Remember, just as the ad's purpose is to persuade readers to send letters, the letter's purpose is to persuade the ad writer to call you. (If you are an advertising executive, you can skip this section.)

There are primarily two main qualities that make for a persuasive letter: flattery and salesmanship. Let's look at each one of these separately.

Flattery - will get you anywhere. Tell the person how wonderful the ad sounded, even if it read like the back of a Cap'n Crunch cereal box. There must be something about the ad you can use flattery on...even if you can only compliment "the excellent way the ad was punctuated with commas and periods." Don't be afraid to say that the author of the ad truly has literary talent.

Salesmanship - Somewhere in your letter you need to give your sales pitch. You need to tell the reader your good qualities and explain how you think you fit the ad's criteria. If the advertiser was looking for someone who is "tall, dark, and handsome" and you are 4'8", pale and look like a frog, for example, you must carefully word your response. Simply state that you are tall, dark, and handsome.

Now you are probably thinking I am recommending that you lie, which is the farthest thing from my mind. Just consider the fact that all adjectives are relative. Take your height for example. Four feet eight inches is tall if you compare yourself to people who are under 4'2" tall. If you look at your complexion relative to an albino, you would be considered "dark." And finally, so what if you look like a frog. Other frogs probably think you are handsome. Maybe if the right person kisses you, you'll turn into a prince. So don't take the criteria too literally.

The key here is to make the reader feel like he or she is the only one you are interested in. This can be achieved by inserting one of the following phrases in the beginning of your letter:

- "I've never responded to a personal ad before..."
- "This is all real new to me, for sure..."
- "Even though your ad was the smallest and most mundane I've ever seen, it was the only one in my age category..."

Placing Your Own Personal Ad

The first thing you must decide is how much you are willing to spend. A large ad will usually stand out among the other ads in a newspaper or magazine and thus should receive a greater response rate. Remember, however, you must have enough money left over to meet whoever responds to your ad.

Once you have decided how much to spend, you need to determine where you will place the ad. Your options probably consist of local newspapers, magazines, singles' newsletters, and religious organizations' bulletins. Your decision will depend on three factors: cost of ad, whom you want to reach, and the size of that audience. The following exercise will help clarify how this works:

PROBLEM:

You have a choice of three publications to place your ad:

Publication - The Chicago Yuppie
Publication type - magazine
Audience type - young professionals, age 24-38
Audience size - 400,000
Cost per line - $45
Minimum - 6 lines ($270)
Cost per impression (person reached) - less than $1

Publication - The U.S. Enquirer
Publication type - newspaper
Audience type - mostly sleazebags
Audience size - 35,000
Cost per line - 50¢
Minimum - 2 lines ($1)
Cost per impression - who cares?

Publication - Singles' World Today
Publication type - newsletter
Audience type - singles age 30-50
Audience size - 320
Cost per line - $2
Minimum - 10 lines ($20)
Cost per impression - 6¢

You have $70 you want to spend on advertising. Which publication should you choose?

ANSWER:

With only $70 you can forget about advertising. Instead, you should have 200 wallet-size pictures made of yourself and list your name and phone number on the back of each one. Then let your mother hand these out to eligible singles she sees in the supermarket.

Now that you have decided where to place your ad and how much to spend, you need only write the ad to complete the process. If writing is not your forte (it surely isn't mine), consider letting your grandmother write the ad. At least you will know she will only write nice things about you. Your grandmother might even foot the bill for the ad in the hopes of finally marrying you off.

Hiring a small advertising agency like Ogilvy & Mather would be the best choice if you have $20,000 to spend on ad development work. Barring that, I will assume you will be writing the ad yourself. Below is a simple form ad for which you can fill in details specific to your own likes and personality. For each of the blank spaces, choose the expression from the corresponding group that best fits.

___(1)___ ___(2)___ ___(3)___ - Age__, warm, sensitive, dynamic, witty, spiritually and artistically inclined. Seeks __(1)__ __(2)__ age _ to _ who enjoys __(4)_ , __(4)__ , __(4)__ , and __(4)_ . Must be easy to be with, intelligent, __(5)__ , __(5)__ and eager to please. Phone/note/photo a must.

(1)	(2)

good-looking
handsome
very handsome
exceedingly handsome
attractive
very, very attractive in
   a natural, non-plastic
   sense
pretty
pretty attractive
captivating
irresistible
cute
yech
	male
	female
	man
	woman
	whatever

(3)
doctor
lawyer
investment banker
real estate tycoon
game show host

(5)
slightly wacky
good-natured
unusually literate
illuminating
shaded with earthtones
spunky
evolved
briskly independent

(4)
candlelight dinners
expensive restaurants
long walks on beaches
country inns
fireplaces on rainy
   days
the Alps, Caribbean
cattle rustling

Now that you have placed your personal ad, all you need to do now is sit back and wait for those responses to start pouring in. If you followed the above advice on writing and placing the ad, you should receive a minimum of 463 letters in the first three weeks.

But what if you don't get any? Then what? Don't get depressed. First, check your post office to see if you accidently sent in a change of address form to Outer

Mongolia. Second, check to see that you actually sent in the ad to the publication. Third, check the publication to make sure the ad ran. If you have checked all these and they are not the problem, now is the time to get depressed.

For argument's sake, let's assume you have received some responses to your ad. How do you decide whom to call first? The best technique is to use the method most personnel people use for choosing job applicants: Throw all the letters down a flight of stairs and the letter on top is the one to call.

The second best technique is to split the letters into three piles: (1) "Definitely call," (2) "Maybe" and (3) "When hell freezes over." Photocopied form letters always go into pile #3 and letters written in crayon go into pile #1 (anyone who writes in crayon has to be some fun) and letters made from words cut out of various newspapers and magazines should be forwarded to your local police.

The type of stationery used can tell you a great deal about a person. Was the person's personal letterhead used or was it the back of an advertising circular? Was a stamp used on the envelope or a bulk mail indicia?

If the person enclosed a photo, don't necessarily take it at face value (no pun intended). Is it a recent photo or is the person in the photo standing at the 1964 New York World's Fair? Is it a real photo of the person in a sports uniform or a baseball trading card?

Finally, you should consider what they wrote in the letter. It probably won't affect your decision, but you might as well read it anyway.

SECTION III:

Before the Date

Chapter 8
Initial Contact

"Hi Stacey. This is Scott. Karen gave me your number…" "No. That doesn't sound right either."

Where to Call

You first must decide where to call your prospective blind date, if you are given an option. Most of the time you are only given the home phone number. In this case it is probably best to use that one.

If you are given both home and office numbers, start by trying to reach the date at home; you don't want your colleagues at the office to know you are desperate. If you can't reach the person at home after half a dozen tries, use the office number. It is best to call during working hours for this. When you call, say you would have called at home, but you are almost always out at night due to your "busy" social life.

The Opening

Now you are ready to make the call. It is best to use a telephone for this. You must prepare your patter so that you can say it without stuttering or whimpering. It is best if the person is not forewarned of your call by whoever gave you the name—this will make it more challenging.

Always start with "You don't know me, but I'm a friend of so-and-so." This puts the potential blind date at ease, since he or she will figure that you must be okay if the friend gave you the name.

Should you get an answering machine, hang up. If this persists, you will eventually have to leave a message. The difficulty lies in the fact that you will have only 30 seconds to explain that you are a friend of a cousin of a mutual friend whom you met in the seat next to you at a doubleheader baseball game in Chicago while you were there at a water buffalo convention.

The Middle

Now that you have broken the ice and explained to your prospective date exactly how you got the number (assuming it wasn't from a stall in the bathroom in the bus terminal), it is time to carry on the conversation. An easy beginning is to ask about your potential date's job and where he or she lives. These are easy subjects to discuss unless, of course, the person was just fired this afternoon or just evicted from his or her apartment.

In this case say your dinner is burning in the oven and you will call back in a few days (or a few years).

Hopefully, conversation is free-flowing and you can ad-lib from here. Do *not* make judgements about this person from the phone call. When people speak on the phone for the first time, they are usually not at ease and can project a very different image from their real personality, unless of course, you are speaking to Ricardo Montalban. (He can make "Corinthian leather" sound sexy.)

The Close—Going for Broke

If you can ascertain from the phone conversation that this one gets the big "L" (loser), you can always end it by saying you are very busy with your career (you are working on a merger deal between IBM and Apple Computer) and will call to arrange a date as soon as your work load lightens up, say in 1995. This is the chicken's way out. (Don't just sit there clucking! Read on!)

Your best move is to ask the person out and use it for experience. It will offer an added benefit of giving you a good story to tell your friends and co-workers at the office. If, however, this would be your seventh blind date this month, don't waste your time (you've already wasted it six times).

The "close" is relatively easy, once you know the secret. When the conversation begins to lull or when your phone bill reaches double-digits, go for the jugular. Say something like, "Listen, why don't we get together sometime?" If the potential date responds with

"I'd rather see King Kong," gracefully get out of it by saying, "Fine, we'll go see a science fiction movie."

If the person is somewhat more responsive, which you can figure out by a simple "Sure, I'd love to get together," ask him or her out for whatever date you have planned. You have just successfully completed the initial contact.

Chapter 9
Where and When to Go on the Date

"Well, what did you have in mind?"

Time and Place

After you get the name, you must decide where to meet. The most important thing to remember is to minimize your risk. If your blind date looks like a perfect "10," you are all set no matter where you meet. However, if your date looks more like The Incredible Hulk, you need a place that will make the meeting as painless as possible. Here are a few suggestions:

A Movie

A movie is an excellent choice for a blind date as it offers an inexpensive evening with limited conversation required so you won't have to repeat your life story to her. A movie theater has an added benefit of being dark, so there is little chance of being seen with your blind date by any of your friends.

Horror films are good as long as you don't scream louder than your date. If your date did not understand the plot to "Conan the Destroyer," try not to pick a movie in which you will be answering questions for two hours. This will limit your choices, however, to "Bambi" and "Rocky IX." A comedy is good for breaking the ice between you and your date. Any film starring Arnold Schwartzenegger or Chuck Norris should have you both rolling in the aisles.

When choosing a movie, the location of the theater is as important as the choice of movie. The theater should be located as close to your date's home as possible so that you don't have to make awkward conversation for too long on the way to the theater.

The type of theater is also important. You can either go to a drive-in or walk-in theater. A drive-in theater is fine as long as your car has automatic transmission. Otherwise, if you are planning any sort of passionate interlude during the movie credits, you might be spending the following morning in a proctologist's office having a stick shift surgically removed. Alternatively, don't just show up at your blind date's door with a box of Milk Duds and a video cassette of "Pee Wee Herman's Big Adventure" under your arm; your date may not like Milk Duds.

If your date seems worthwhile and you are willing to risk conversation, you can always go out for drinks afterwards. If not, you can just end the date there.

Lunch

Lunch should be your first choice on a blind date. It puts the date at ease, as it is during daylight hours in a situation that is considered "safe." More important, however, it allows for a quick exit if the date turns out to be a bore. You may simply say that you have an important meeting with your company president. This can cut lunch down to twenty minutes if you are good (choose a restaurant with fast service).

If the situation is really desperate, tell your date you have to go put more change in the parking meter and then do not return. This is worth trying even if you don't own a car.

If the date is a real dud, ask for a corner table in the smoking section (this is usually in the back of the restaurant); if you don't want any of your friends to see you, never choose a restaurant where you might be recognized.

Coffee

Meeting the blind date for a cup of coffee is also very good. It is much less expensive than lunch. If you bring your own tea bag, you can probably get away for under $1.00.

The coffee meeting can be cut down to ten minutes if necessary. You can easily have three dates in the evening if two of them are for coffee. (Of course, you will spend the entire evening excusing yourself to go to the rest room).

Drinks

Meeting a blind date for drinks is not recommended unless it is done immediately after work. Drinks can last all evening, which could be disastrous. If your date is a real bomb, with your luck he or she most likely can drink like a fish and will want to spend the entire evening with you. The worse the date is, the more time that person will want to spend with you.

There is only one solution: drink heavily. Do not waste time on beer or wine...go straight for the bourbon. WARNING: Do not drink so much that your date starts to look cute and sound interesting. If this happens, take no chances—say you have a breakfast meeting a week from Thursday with your boss at work and need to get home early to prepare; you don't like waiting until the last minute.

The best time for drinks is around 5PM. If your date is somewhat fun and exciting, you can always go out for dinner. If not, you can leave early for a fictitious dinner engagement.

Dinner

Dinner should be arranged only if you can't meet for lunch. Most important is to never, I repeat, NEVER let your date choose the restaurant unless you are independently wealthy. Many a person's rent money went into one dinner with a boring date.

If by chance you are a jerk and let your date choose the restaurant, there is a way out. When you arrive at the restaurant and realize there is valet parking, do not panic. The most important thing to remember is that pride is only relative.

You probably agreed to the type of restaurant, so telling your date that you are allergic to French food won't work at this point. Say that you did not realize this was the same restaurant your father was suing for breach of contract. "It has something to do with a limited partnership tax shelter deal. I don't totally understand the details, but it would probably be better if we didn't eat here." (This situation once happened to me and I managed to get away for only $217 not including the tip). So you see, it can be done.

While dinner is definitely not the best choice for a blind date, many times it is the only time to get together. If this is the case, you must use the patented "Three Restaurant Backup Technique." This technique relies on your ability to think quickly on your feet—sizing up your date in the first three minutes of meeting and choosing the best restaurant.

Restaurant #1 is a very small, candlelit, out-of-the-way place with soft music in the background. This is perfect for the person who at first impression seems potentially like the date of your dreams.

Restaurant #2 is a very big, loud and fun place with waiters and waitresses who sing and dance in the aisles. This is perfect for the person who seems like a lot of fun on a date.

Restaurant #3 is a very small, candlelit, out-of-the-way place with counter service only. This is perfect for the person who does not fit into either of the above two categories. The counter service makes the meal quick and has the added benefit of not forcing you to look at each other at all during dinner (make sure the counter does not have mirrors behind it).

Because the cost of blind dating was starting to get out of hand, (It's amazing how my dates always go to the bathroom just when the check arrives—For years I thought women had incredibly weak bladders), my friend Bob Finkle and I developed the perfect solution—the Fin-Nagel Blind Date Credit Card:

FIN-NAGEL **BLIND DATE CREDIT CARD**
Jeffrey S. Nagel 8765 4321 100   Exp 10/95

This card should be presented to the waiter when he hands you the bill. He will immediately tell you the restaurant does not accept the Fin-Nagel card. You then show some fake embarrassment to your date and say that is the only credit card you brought and you only have $5 in cash. Ask your date to pick up the check and you will pay next time. This method should help you finagle your way out of buying dinner.

If, on the other hand, you were asked out to dinner, you would expect your date to pay. When the check comes, don't even acknowledge its existence. Instead, your best bet is to excuse yourself until the whole distasteful chore of paying the bill is taken care of by your date.

Suppose the check comes and your date doesn't reach for it. As a matter of fact your date not only doesn't acknowledge its existence, but gets up and goes to the bathroom. Now what do you do? Don't sweat—you haven't paid for a meal in years and you sure as hell don't want to ruin a good streak now.

When your date returns from the bathroom, simply ask him one of the following questions:

- "Did you take care of the check while you were gone?"
- "You don't want any money, DO YOU?"
- "If you are going to charge the bill to your credit card, can I have the receipt for tax purposes?"
- (Or if you are feeling magnanimous) "Do you want me to leave the tip?"

If after using one of the above lines your date still has the audacity to ask you to split the bill, start speaking in a foreign language, pretending you no longer understand English.

The Day of the Week

Thursday night is a poor choice since there is usually something more interesting on TV than an evening with a blind date. The best day of the week for a blind date is a Monday or Tuesday. This offers you the opportunity of going out again for the weekend if your date turns out to be real interesting. On the other hand, if your date turns out to be a dud, you haven't wasted a weekend night. Also, you have an excuse to end the evening early since you have to work the next day. (If you are presently unemployed, disregard this reasoning.)

Places Not to Go

Knowing where *not* to go is just as important as knowing where to go. To help you with this I have listed a few places to skip over when deciding on an outing for your next blind date:

Deep sea fishing	• The smell of live bait in the morning will turn your stomach quicker than the sight of your blind date.
Zoos	• One of the Urangutans might hit on your date while you are feeding a baboon. (I was *not* referring to your date.)
Your parents' house	• If they are like most parents, they will try to arrange a wedding right there on the spot.
Flea markets	• Nothing is more embarrassing than walking by a clothing booth with your date and seeing the outfit you are wearing on sale for $6.
Rifle ranges	• You do not want to be in the same room with a blind date and a gun in your hand.
Outdoor Wine tastings	• It is very difficult trying to impress someone when you miss the ground and spit wine all over their shoes.

Instead of these places, you decide to meet your blind date at an art auction. This will at least show that you are a sophisticated and cultured person...until you scratch your nose, inadvertently causing you to purchase a Ming vase worth $3.2 million. Unfortunately, the Fin-Nagel Blind Date Credit Card won't get you out of this one, nor will the fact that your place is decorated in early Ethan Allen. If you must go to an auction, stick with one where the most expensive item is comparable to the value of the old camp trunk in your parents' attic.

Chapter 10
How to Prepare for the Date

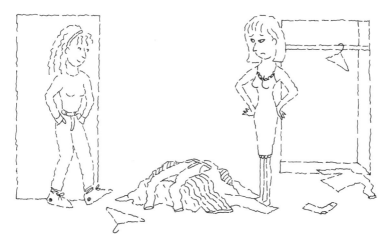

"Blind date tonite?"

What to Bring

You have been on hundreds of dates in the past; so why do you need to read about what to bring on a date? Well, a blind date is not like any date you have ever been on before. You have never met this person so you need to be prepared for anything. What if your date has no sense of humor? What if you get stranded at a restaurant and need to find your own way home? What if your date is all hands?

On the next page is a list of the contents of a basic Blind Date Survival Kit™. You should carry these items with you at all times on your first date:

ITEM	PURPOSE
Money	• To pay for your share of dinner in case he or she expects something in return.
Credit cards	• To get back into your own apartment if you lose your keys.
Fin-Nagel Blind Date Credit Card	• In case you get stuck with the check.
Breath freshener	• In case your date has bad breath (don't be embarrassed to ask him to use this).
Disinfectant	• You'll know if you need this item.
A Camera	• To capture the moment, since no one is going to believe this.
Running shoes	• For those quick exits.
A beeper	• To get you out of a bad situation for an "emergency."
Spare auto parts	• For fixing your car if it breaks down and your date is a dud (even if you aren't driving).
A book	• Something to read in case your date is boring.
The Blind Date Survival Guide	• To steer you through those rough waters.
A baseball bat	• In case your date takes those AT&T ads literally.

What Not to Bring

During my early days of blind dating, I always brought a single flower, usually a red rose, for my date. Because of the large volume of flowers I was purchasing from Bruce's Flower Shop, my local florist, Bruce, arranged a line of credit for me. This worked out quite well until 1982-83 when interest rates soared. I was paying over $700 in interest charges alone. (That works out to $273.48 worth of flowers each month.)

Although my dates were impressed by the flowers, the expense was getting out of hand. (Actually, it was usually the date's friends who were more impressed by the flower than the date herself.) The final breaking point was one Sunday in May. I was meeting a woman named Carol in front of the Museum of Natural History for brunch. Since I had never met her before, she gave me her description as 5'4", brown hair, and wearing a white top.

I arrived at the meeting place with rose in hand and sat on the steps outside the museum waiting for another chapter of this book to arrive. A very attractive woman came from inside the museum behind me and sat down nearby.

She fit the bill to a T and I was pleasantly surprised. So I asked her if her name was Carol. Not a chance.

Just then I saw a woman walking across the street toward the museum. She was about 5'4", had brown hair, and was wearing a white top. That is where the similarity with the woman sitting nearby ended. The woman walking toward me was very "punked out" and had neglected to mention little details like her brown hair was streaked with lines of blue and orange. Her clothes looked like they had not been washed since Woodstock. So I took the flower and gave it to the woman sitting next to me instead of my blind date before she was close enough to see. That was the last flower I (almost) gave on a blind date. (Well, what would you have done?)

NOTE: After you have had at least your first date with someone, bringing a single rose is always appreciated and very classy. This also has the added benefit of making the person wonder who got the other eleven.

The Confirming Call

It is hard enough to go on a blind date. You don't want to be rejected (i.e. stood up) before you even meet. Wait until after you meet to be rejected.

A day or two prior to your date, call to confirm the time and place of your meeting. Suppose your potential date suddenly had to go out of town on business, lost your phone number, couldn't remember your last name to get it from information, and is no longer on speaking terms with the person who fixed you both up? Yes, this could actually happen.

Leaving for the Date

What time to leave? There are basically three options: leave so that you arrive on time, leave so that you arrive late, or leave so that you arrive early. (You really needed a book to tell you this, didn't you?!)

Arriving on Time

If you attempt to arrive pretty much on time, you would have to know the exact directions to her house (assuming you are meeting there), driving time, mileage, traffic and weather conditions and how they would affect driving time. Even with all this information required, you still decide to attempt this feat.

So, the day prior to your blind date, with driving directions in hand, you set off to her house for a "dry run." Say, for example, it takes you 28 minutes to get there and 25 minutes to return home. Not enough data for a statistical t-test, but enough to get an average. In addition to this information you know that when the traffic reports speak of 20-minute delays on the thruway, there is usually an extra 8-minute delay no matter where you are going. Also, when there is a snow-fall of 2 inches at 29 degrees Fahrenheit, your car will take an extra 3 minutes to start with a 17-minute delay in driving time.

The night of the date you listen to the radio to hear about a 35-minute delay on the thruway with a temperature of 31 degrees and a 3 inch snowfall. Plugging this information into the following equation (it's best to use an IBM mainframe computer), you can determine the exact time to leave your home:

t_g	=	driving time going to her house from dry run	= 28
t_r	=	driving time returning home from dry run	= 25
S_e	=	expected snowfall in inches	= 3
R_e	=	expected rainfall in inches	= 0
T	=	temperature in degrees Fahrenheit	= 31
d	=	delay on thruway in minutes	= 35
m	=	mileage between your place and hers	= 18
S_s	=	standard snowfall in inches	= 2

d_s = delay due to snowfall in minutes = 17

Ts = standard temperature in degrees Fahrenheit = 29

d_a = delay due to auto start-up in minutes = 3

t_d = time of date = 7pm

F = fudge factor =.003

t_e = time to leave house

$$t_e = t_d - \frac{(t_g + t_r)^d/2 + d_s \times [m - 7]^{\,da}}{(S_e^T - S_s^{Ts})^3 \times R_e} + F$$

As you can see from the above example, you would have to leave at 6:32pm to arrive at your date's house on time.

Arriving Late

The second option, arriving late, should not become your normal practice as it is discourteous. Of course if your date turns out to be a bomb, you have managed to kill 15 minutes by being that much late.

If you do arrive late, however, it is best to use one of the following excuses:

a) "I thought you said make a *right* on Main street. I knew it was kind of strange when I crossed the state line." or

b) "I got here on time, but I'm driving a new car and couldn't figure out how to get the key out of the ignition."

If you are more than three hours late, call your date and pretend she was to meet you at your apartment. When she questions you on why you asked for directions to her house, say that you wanted directions for the florist so they could deliver flowers.

Arriving Early

The third option, arriving early, makes you appear too eager...as if you had nothing better to do on a Saturday night. Who's kidding whom? That's exactly why you are going on the blind date—you *don't* have anything better to do.

Now while arriving early is quite acceptable, try to limit this to two hours or less. Anything more than that could go beyond eager and fall into the desperate category.

SECTION IV:

The Date

Chapter 11
That Magic Moment...Maybe

First Impression

This is the moment of truth. You are about to meet your blind date. Any minute now you will be face to face with a total stranger with whom you will be spending the next few hours. Various questions will probably run through your mind as you wait with anticipation: Will he be cute? Will she be smart? Will he be fun to be with? Will she have a sense of humor? Is it too late to back out of this?

When nobody is looking, you nonchalantly put your hand up to your mouth and blow into it to see if your breath smells. Then you take a couple of sniffs and real-

---

ize you put on too much perfume. You probably should have changed your outfit when you spilled the bottle on your blouse, but you were running too late to do anything about it. If you are lucky, your date will have a sinus condition and not even notice.

You glance across the room and see her. She is easy to pick out because she is doing the "Blind Date Scan." This is a method of looking around a room, trying to guess which person is the blind date. She spots a sexy-looking guy in the corner staring at her. Hoping he is the one, she starts to walk toward him, at which point his wife returns from the ladies' room and puts her arms around him.

Eventually, your eyes meet and you both mouth the other person's name without actually saying a word. (You do this so no one else in the room will know it's a blind date.) You both introduce yourselves and decide right then whether you are going to enjoy the evening. Well, he's not exactly what you expected. Somehow you pictured him as a little taller. But at least he doesn't have a big gap between his front teeth like your last blind date. Whenever there was a breeze, his teeth would make a high-pitched whistling sound, causing every dog and cat in the neighborhood to follow him around.

She is slightly heavier than you expected, but she does have a pleasant face. And you were hoping for bigger, uh, "lungs," but you were never too good at those new-fangled front bra straps anyway.

Bait and Switch

When your blind date arrives at the door, you can take quick control of the situation by having already chosen the restaurant. The key, of course, is to talk your date into going to the restaurant you chose instead of one of the three dives he or she has in mind (see Chapter 9).

Before your date has a chance to say anything, a comment such as this should do the trick: "Oh, hi! I hope you don't mind, but I've made reservations at a restaurant for us because my friends told me this place was excellent and I've been looking forward to eating there for months and when you called to ask me out, I thought this would be the perfect time to try out the restaurant and I've heard so many good things about it...You don't mind, DO YOU?!!!"

If your date has the nerve to recommend one of the three "choice" restaurants after your soliloquy, simply say it was closed down yesterday by the Board of Health.

Waiting for Your Date

If you decide to meet your date at a restaurant and arrive early, you have a dilemma: Should you stand inside by the front entrance, hang out at the bar, or ask to be seated at your table?

You could wait by the front entrance. Since not many people usually wait there, your blind date should easily be able to spot you, despite the particularly vague description you gave of yourself. Here you are standing in the open where everybody in the restaurant can see you. No one will know that you are early—they will figure your date is late and wonder whether you are being stood up.

You could hang out at the bar. There you could relax with a Perrier with a twist or a double scotch, depending on your nerves. The swizzle stick served with your drink will give your hands something to do instead of constantly putting them in and out of your pockets, just to keep busy. And who knows, you may meet someone you like better!

Finally, you could ask to be seated at your table and wait for your date there. The entire restaurant won't be staring at you and you don't have to try to make conversation with anybody while you are waiting. But what do you do with yourself to keep busy? Think about errands you have to run over the weekend? Plan your schedule for the next couple of days? And you always have to keep looking at your watch and glancing toward the entrance, just so that the nosy couple at the table next to you doesn't think you are dining alone.

How to Check out Your Date and Skip the Meeting

If you are squeamish about the blind date and want to check him out first, there is a simple method for doing this. When calling him for the first time, arrange to get together for either lunch or for a drink after work and meet him there.

Ask him what he looks like and what he will be wearing so you will be able to recognize him. Then describe yourself and be very specific about what you will be wearing. Obviously, do not wear anything that remotely resembles what you have described.

On the day of the meeting arrive fifteen minutes early and look around for someone with his description. When he shows up and is cute, you can always explain that your green skirt and orange plaid blouse you said you'd be wearing were at the cleaners, which is why you are wearing a Royal blue dress instead. If he turns out looking like a chapter in Darwin's theory of evolution, you can always duck out the exit and then vanish from the face of the earth. (I don't really recommend this method as it gives blind dating a bad name.)

CAUTION: If your date shows up wearing something totally different from what he described, he obviously read this book and had the same thing in mind.

In the Car with Your Date

Now that you are past the formalities of the introductions and initial small talk, you both hop into your car (if you are meeting at her place) and head to your destination. At this point conversation could get awkward, so it is best to have the radio on to fill in the lulls. If you don't have a radio, improvise with your own singing (this will also test her sense of humor).

Suppose you see right away that this date is going downhill fast. You will not want to waste a lot of time sitting in your car with her, so your goal then becomes reaching your destination as quickly as possible. Nonchalantly take your racing gloves and helmet out of the glove compartment and put them on. If your date questions this, just say that they give you a sense of security.

Then shift into fifth gear, put your foot to the floor, and close all the windows to reduce drag. Neglect all red lights along the way, unless, of course, they are flashing in conjunction with a siren. Try to refrain from blurting out comments like, "Pilot to copilot" when addressing your date. The above course of action should dramatically reduce your driving time.

NOTE: If your date offers to take a cab and meet you at the destination instead of riding with you, she either does not want to be seen with you or is afraid of fast cars. If you are driving a Hyundai, you might want to check your appearance in the rear view mirror.

What to Talk About

When you first meet, there are definitely things you should not say.

INSTEAD OF SAYING ...	SAY ...
My friend didn't tell me you were so fat.	• Gee, I thought you'd be a lot heavier.
My friend didn't tell me you were so stupid.	• It's okay, I'll talk slow and won't use any words over two syllables.
My friend didn't tell me you were in a car accident.	• Your face couldn't stop a Mack truck.
My friend didn't tell me you were so boring.	• Too many people put importance on good conversation.

In general, you should follow these guidelines:

SUBJECTS TO DISCUSS:	SUBJECTS TO AVOID:
• your job	• your date's job
• your family	• your date's family
• your achievements	• your date's achievements
• your past girlfriends/boyfriends	• your date's past boyfriends/girlfriends
• your career goals	• your date's career goals

These subjects may bore your date, but you like hearing yourself speak anyway. Actually, the key to the successful blind date is conversation. This is the means by which you get to know each other. If your life story is not that interesting, feel free to use someone else's experiences as if they were your own. (How do you think I got all the anecdotes for this book?!)

What Not to Eat or Drink

It is your first date and of course you want to make a good impression. So ordering a Shirley Temple from the bar before dinner or a glass of warm milk as an after-dinner drink will most likely not give you that worldly appearance you so wanted to project.

When it comes to food, there is only one major rule: Don't order anything that has a 99% chance of ending up on your lap. To begin with, that cuts out spaghetti. If the sauce doesn't hit you while you are twirling the spaghetti onto your fork (the tablespoon is useless), you will invariably end up with a two-foot strand stretching from your plate to your mouth.

Lobster is out. First of all, you have to wear a plastic bib with a giant picture of a lobster on it. With this on don't even attempt a serious conversation until coffee and dessert. And then it is only a matter of time before you accidently squirt lemon juice in your date's eye.

Forget about soup. First of all, you and I both know there is no way in the world to eat soup without making that slurping sound. And when you do, you kind of look down at your spoon, you make that slurping sound, and then you realize you made that slurping sound. You don't want to look up because your date is staring at you for making the sound. And chances are, when you get to the bottom of the bowl, you are going to pick up the bowl and slurp the rest of it. Trust me on this one— skip the soup.

Salads usually come with most meals and are good for the digestion anyway. What you have to watch out for, though, are those little red cherry tomatoes. The atomic bomb was designed after these. You can't cut them with a knife and fork because the minute you reach for them they will go flying across the table. Your only option is to put them in your mouth whole. That's the easy part.

The tricky part is chewing them. You've got this red ping pong ball in your mouth, which you try to maneuver over to the side teeth without distorting your face too much as you do it. You move it around with your tongue until you get it into just the right position between your teeth. At this point your mouth is wide open to accommodate this projectile. As you start to bite down on the tomato, your date sees the impending danger and dives for cover under the table before a stream of tomato juice squirts across the table. Need I say more?

If you go out for nouvelle cuisine, do not order the lamb chops. They will make those cherry tomatoes look like a six course meal. When your main course arrives you will be served two lamb chops sitting in the center of a plate the size of the one you use to carve a Thanksgiving turkey. The lamb will be surrounded by garnishes on all sides to fill up the empty portions of your plate. You look down and see two, maybe three, bites tops before you finish your dinner.

After finishing those few morsels, you are dying to munch on the bones, but restrain yourself because you are in public with a blind date. Your only hope is to create a diversion so you can finish your meal. You casually reach across the table for your water glass and "accidentally" knock the salt shaker off the table in your date's direction. As your date leans over to pick it up, you quickly grab for one of your bones and start gnawing on it until there is nothing left. You then throw it back on your plate before your date gets back up from the floor. The question then is, Do you have the nerve to knock over the pepper shaker to get to your other bone?

In addition, it is wise to stay away from sardines, garlic bread (unless hoping to prevent the good night kiss), chili (or anything else that could cause a gastronomical explosion in your body), anything you can't pronounce, and anything you can't tell if it's animal, vegetable, or mineral.

How to Avoid the Good Night Kiss and More

Well, the date has just about come to an end. If it is an afternoon date, most likely a good-bye kiss would not come up. So let us assume you are less than thrilled with your date and you are going home at the end of a long evening, say at 8 o'clock. You want to avoid the good night kiss at all costs. There are a couple of things you can do in this situation, assuming you did not already chew on a clove of garlic sometime during the evening.

[**For men**]: First, when you stop the car, quickly jump out and walk her to the door. Otherwise, you will have to say good night to her inside your car, which is awkward and will invariably lead to a kiss—she might not leave until you give her one.

So you walk her up to the door and she puts the key in the lock. There is a good chance she is signaling that she wants you to come in. At this point you should let out the biggest yawn you can and excuse yourself saying you didn't get much sleep last night. As she opens the door, take one step back and put your hands in your pockets (most men put their hands on a woman while kissing her), and tell her you had a nice evening. Say "good night," turn around and head for your car, waving as you do so. When you reach your car, let out a sigh of relief.

[**For women**]: If your date is really bad news, see if you can cause your nose to bleed. No one will want to kiss you while you are standing there with your head tilted back, dripping blood all over his handkerchief. If you can't stand the sight of blood (especially your own) or you had your nose done when you were thirteen, I have provided an alternate method.

As he is walking you to your door, make sure that you are at least a couple of steps ahead of him (even if you have to break into a sprint). When you reach your door, step toward it with your right foot and pivot on your left, holding out your right hand for a handshake. By doing this maneuver, you have placed a good two feet between your lips and his. For him to kiss you he would have to either step on your left foot or climb up your knee; in which case you are in a position to use that knee to make sure he remembers you every time he sings in the choir.

As you are holding out your hand, simply say, "With all the germs going around these days, why don't we just end the date on an up note with a handshake?!" This, and your knee, should end his thoughts of getting a good night kiss.

"I'll call you..."

Most men at the end of a date will invariably say, "I'll call you," whether they mean it or not. While some might consider this an inherited trait, I believe it is actually a reflex action...like saying "God bless you" after someone sneezes. Someone sneezes—you say "God bless you." The date ends—you say "I'll call you." See?! It's a reflex.

The difficulty arises from the fact that the end of the first date can be very awkward. What do you say if you are not interested in seeing this person again? "Goodbye. Have a nice life." "Please forgive me if I don't call you again, but I had a miserable time." Somehow these lines don't work. A simple "good-bye" seems to beg for something to go with it. It just doesn't stand on its own.

There is a solution, of course. If you are not interested in seeing this person again, simply say "Thank you for a lovely evening. While I had a very nice time, I think you would enjoy dating my friend Igor more than me. He is a very nice guy. Would you mind if I gave him your phone number?" (For this to work you must have a friend Igor who is always willing to go out with just about anybody).

SECTION V:

After the Date

Chapter 12
The Follow Up

*"You probably expect something in return for taking me out to dinner
and a show. Hold on and I'll give you a receipt."*

Good Time

The blind date is over. And you made it through
relatively unscathed. As a matter of fact, you might
even say you had a good time. Now what have you
learned from that? For one thing, you know that the person who fixed you up had pretty good taste (unless that
person gave you a streak of bozos prior to this one). So
you know it is probably worthwhile to get other names
from this person.

Another thing you have learned is that the techniques outlined in this book actually work. That's right. I didn't make them all up just to fill space, you know.

Anyway, it is important to get in touch with the blind date broker within a week to give a report on how the date went and to offer thanks for the name and phone number. (Leave out the details.) This is necessary since it gives respectability to the blind dating profession and is just downright courteous.

Let's say you had a super time. She was witty, charming—everything you could ever hope for. So you call her again and arrange a second date, expecting another enchanting evening. But on the second date you are totally bored. Her charm is gone and her wit is a thing of the past. This couldn't be the same woman you went out with a week ago. What happened?

Maybe she had only one good date in her. Suppose she had just enough wit and charm for a first date. She could last six, maybe eight, hours at best if she had to, but that was it. Afterwards, she reverts back to her old boring self. (This phenomenon is analyzed in more detail in the December issue of some psychological journal or other.)

Bad Time

The blind date is over. And it didn't turn out exactly as you thought it would. (Does it ever?) On the phone your date sounded like so much fun; he laughed at all your jokes and seemed very interested in your career. Besides which, he sounded very sexy.

But when you met at the restaurant, he asked for separate tables. (What a kidder!) During dinner he kept yawning when you talked about your job as a quality control inspector in a fertilizer plant. Each time you said something funny he just looked at his watch and said, "My, how late it is!" The only time he laughed was when you asked if he would like to see you again. What should you do? Forget about him—he probably doesn't like your favorite sport, watermelon seed spitting, anyway.

If your date was terrible, but persists in calling you...

- Call to say you are leaving the country.
- Call to say your phone number changed and give the number of the Chinese laundry across the street.
- Legally change your name.
- Get plastic surgery.
- Enter the Government Witness Protection Program.
- Join the Peace Corps.

Chapter 13

For the Seasoned Professional

"I've got 3 blind dates tonite. Drinks with Steffi at 5:30, dinner with Debbie at 7:00, and coffee with Marsha at 9:00...No Problem—I timed it perfectly."

OK. So you've read this book cover to cover and you consider yourself a seasoned professional. You've been to more cheap restaurants than your stomach could stand and you've seen the same lousy movies so many times you know the projectionists by name.

It isn't that you are fed up with blind dating. You don't even mind that feeling of anticipation when meeting your blind date for the first time (kind of like opening the results of your driver's test to see if you passed).

What you really hate more than anything is when your date uses that old, worn-out remark, "So tell me about yourself."

You have had a blind date for lunch and a different one for drinks after work before you meet your present date, who has the nerve to ask what you do for a living. "How many brothers and sisters do you have? Do you like your job? Where did you grow up? Have you traveled much? What do your folks do?" Ad nauseam.

Wouldn't it be nice not to have to go through all of that? Your date really doesn't care about your answers anyway. However, there is a solution to this problem...Now! From the people who brought you the Fin-Nagel Card, the new and exciting: Canned Resume! Never tell another blind date how long you've been a cashier in the supermarket. No longer will you lose your voice explaining why you ran away from home at age four.

Just type your life history on a piece of white paper and have it reduced to the size of a business card. Then have 500 copies made and give them to your blind dates when you meet them.

BLIND DATE RESUME
Jeffrey S. Nagel

Date of Birth: 04/09/59
Residence: New York
Brothers: 1 married, 2 children (1 boy, 1 girl)
Sisters: 3 married, 2 children each (4 boys, 2 girls)
Education: B.S. Cornell University
    M.B.A. University of Michigan
Hobbies: reading, cooking, art
Sports: tennis, skiing, golf, racquetball, volleyball
Analyst: Dr. Sigmund Freud
Plumber: Phil Cooper
Life Goals: to become president of General Motors or IBM. If not, to be a soda jerk.
Greatest Fears: snakes, blind dates

Chapter 14
Conclusion

"Would you please speak up. It has taken me 237 blind dates to get here and I don't want my mom to miss a word."

After being in the singles' scene for only a short period of time you realize it is definitely not all it's cracked up to be. In more concise terms: It Stinks. Valentine's Day rolls around and the only one you have to send flowers to is mom. You go to a wedding solo and everyone says, "You mean you are here ALONE?!!"

This book pokes fun at blind dating because it is the best way of dealing with the singles' scene. Instead of getting depressed about having another lousy blind date, try to find something humorous in the situation. Maybe you forgot her name when she answered the door or maybe the only place you had to put the rose he brought you was in an empty jar of Milk of Magnesia. The key is to keep things in perspective and laugh about them. Remember: **LIFE IS TOO IMPORTANT TO TAKE SERIOUSLY.**

Chapter 15
The Best (or Worst) Blind Date Contest

"This is definitely the worst blind date story ever. What a loser that date was."

Do you have a great blind date story? Would you like to win valuable prizes? I'd like to hear about it, no matter how the date turned out. The date with the best story will be given a set of matching salt and pepper shakers and will appear in the second edition of this book. *Just send me a summary of your date addressed to:

BLIND DATE CONTEST
Blockbuster Publishing, Inc.
P.O. Box 415-BDC
Greenvale, NY 11548

by December 31, 1989 to be eligible. Here is a sample letter I already received:

> Dear Jeff,
>
> Last week I went on a blind date with a doctor. He was supposed to pick me up and take me out to dinner. When he arrived, he told me he was in the middle of an autopsy and asked me if I minded watching.
>
> After about an hour of watching him cut some guy up, I left and went home.
>
> Sincerely,
>
> Disgusted

Do you have a better story? Let me know.

---

*All stories received will become the property of the publisher with all rights to publish them.

Epilogue

During the pre-publication publicity campaign, I spoke to numerous newspaper and magazine editors, trying to promote this guide. For three weeks I wined and dined people with the hopes of getting this book mentioned in articles. It didn't work, but I did manage to gain five pounds.

Then I got a call from an editor of my hometown newspaper, Michelle, who heard about the guide and wanted to interview me over dinner. Having eaten out for twenty-three nights straight, I asked if she would mind doing the interview over a home-cooked meal. She refused to cook, so I opted to play chef for an evening.

Michelle came over to my apartment to a candlelight dinner with a single red rose on the table and a bottle of 1971 Chateaux Margaux. I served stuffed mushrooms as an appetizer, steamed artichokes for the first course, an endive salad, and duck à l'orange for the main course with a vegetable trio and rice pilaf. For dessert I made crêpes suzette. (Actually, the crêpes came out lumpy, so we ended up having "glop" suzette.)

While the interview never got printed, the evening was a success. And you thought this guide didn't work. (For what it's worth, I've included the recipe.)

Duck à l'Orange

1 duck
pinch of pepper
pinch of salt
2 oranges
smidgen of cornstarch
handful of sugar
swig of brandy
2 bottles red bordeaux

1. Serve first bottle of wine to your guests.

2. Clean duck and place on rack in open roasting pan. Roast at 350°F. for 2 hours.

3. Serve second bottle of wine.

4. *While duck is cooking, prepare sauce:* Squeeze juice from one orange, add a little water and the rest of the ingredients. Heat in saucepan until sugar melts.

5. Serve duck with sauce poured on top, surrounded by wild rice and thin orange slices.